Love In The "In-Between"

Unspoken Words

Dr Souvik Roy

BookLeaf Publishing

India | USA | UK

Made with ❤ on the BookLeaf Publishing Platform
www.bookleafpub.in
www.bookleafpub.com

Dedication

To my lovely people and the love that shaped these words.
And a special mention to Bunny, who made the in-between moments unforgettable.

Preface

Love in the "In-Between" is a collection of poems about love, friendship, longing, and the emotions that shape our relationships. It explores the space between joy and sorrow, closeness and distance, spoken words and unspoken feelings.

Love has always fascinated me—it is both beautiful and unpredictable. It lifts us to incredible heights and, at times, breaks us apart. Yet, we keep searching for it, trying to understand its mysteries.

These poems are my way of capturing those emotions—the ones we feel deeply but don't always say out loud. Some are drawn from personal moments, others from the world around me, but all reflect the connections that make us human.

Poetry has a way of reaching straight to the heart. My hope is that within these pages, you'll find a piece of your own story—something that makes you feel seen, understood, and maybe even a little less alone.

Thank you for reading. I hope these words find a home in you.

With love,
Souvik.

Acknowledgements

Writing Love in the "In-Between" has been a journey of emotions, reflections, and countless moments of inspiration. This book would not have been possible without the support, love, and encouragement of many people.

First, my heartfelt gratitude to my lovely People, who have always believed in me, even when I doubted myself. Your unwavering support has been my greatest strength.

To my readers—thank you for giving my words a home in your hearts. Your love for poetry and the connections you find in these pages make this journey worthwhile.

A special thank you to everyone who inspired these poems, knowingly or unknowingly. Love, in all its forms, is the greatest muse.

And finally, to those who embrace the beauty of the in-between moments in life—this book is for you.

With gratitude,
Souvik.

1. Love in the "In-Between"

We tread the same paths, yet worlds apart,
Bound by a love we can't let start.
Our stories entwined in fate's cruel thread,
Close enough to long, yet left unsaid.

Your laughter lingers in silent air,
A whispered vow, a fleeting prayer.
Not every love is meant to be,
Yet still, you live inside of me.

In stolen moments, our hearts still speak,
A bond unbroken, though futures seem bleak.
Neither lovers nor strangers, we occupy between,
A fondness unseen, yet deeply keen.

No pledges to keep, no bonds to name,
Yet in my core, you spark the same flame.
For passion's not always meant to last,
But at times, it won't fade into the past.

2. Remember Me, Only in Love

Remember Me, Only in Love
Time flows, never still—
Some return to where memories dwell,
Some seek a warmer heart to rest their weary soul,
Some discover the home of their spirit,
A place where all the joys of their world unfold.
No one lingers, none remain,
Not for anyone, not for long.
Yet, some still wander through fleeting days,
Searching for love's quiet embrace,
A shoulder to lean on,
A haven where the deepest peace resides.
Some will win, some will lose—
A wheel that turns, again and again.
Yet love endures, longing, unshaken,
A whisper that never fades.
So when I vanish into the tides of time,
Remember me—only in love.

3. The Rooftop and the Bitter Coffee

Come then, when you are weary
Of loves that only touch the skin,
When paramours, with passions fiery,
Seek newer flesh, where new delights begin,
And leave you spent, and hollowed deep within.

Come then, when restless hands explore
The prison of your heart's own cage,
When you, from flesh, will seek once more
A love serene, from a bygone age,
A gentle solace on life's empty stage.
Come then—if memory guides your feet!

Come then—and I shall listen, hushed and still,
To tales of raptures, wild and sweet,
That set your very soul athrill,
With passions that your deepest longings fill.

Come then, beneath the starlit skies,
Upon the rooftop, we shall find our peace,
Where silence whispers, as time flies,
Of joys we knew, and sorrows that won't cease,
A tapestry of love, and loss' increase.

Come then—I vow to hear it all!
No ginger-infused tea, so warm and red,
But bitter blackest coffee, I shall call,
And bake for you, instead,
A brew that lingers, even when hope seems dead.

Come then—if you recall the place,
And find me waiting in the self-same spot,
Where bitter coffee fills love's empty space—
Wait there for me, even if I am not,
And love anew, though all else is forgot.

4. Smoke

The one who claimed you, surpassing all my prayers,
On whose chest you rested your head to begin Your Day!
May they keep you safe;
Just as I keep safe, in the torrential rain,
That half-burnt cigarette in my left chest pocket!!

You may forget me, as the mists of ages past Have veiled
those mornings, memories fading fast.
Yet to the emptiness, one day, I shall confide, The tale of
that long night, where shadows did preside,
A solitary journey, down a desolate, winding way,
Where whispers of the lonely hours held sway.

5. UNEASE

Years have passed since our last sight,
Ages since we spoke, day and night.
Now emptiness brings word to me,
You don't recall a memory.

I talked with emptiness awhile,
And asked, despite my forced-back smile,
When last it saw you, free and bold.
It smiled, "At twilight, I behold—
You spoke sweet words in that embrace,
Where Your new love's heart beat, and mine had died."

I asked no more, I sought no more.
Just asked emptiness, "If you see her,
Tell her to take care, and find happiness."

And as it left, a whisper flew,
"Doctor, forget her, and
don't be the reason for her unease."

6. CROSSROADS

We stood at separate crossroads, love's map spread wide,
Your hands held a compass, a promise, a guide.
But how could I ask your starlight to wane,
To shrink from the heavens, to shackle the flame?

Your fire, unyielding, too fierce to confine,
Deserved all the cosmos, not just to be mine.
So with silent farewell and love left untold,
We walked different paths—hearts heavy, yet bold.

Some loves burn brightest, then fade into night,
Not lost, but returning to their own light.
And though we are distant, like stars up above,
We shine in the echoes of once-woven love.

7. Date

Soft whispers of a sunset fade,
Our hands entwined, hearts beating as one made.
Theatre's thrill, Ganga's gentle breeze,
Uber's silence, shattered by tender squeeze.

A kiss, a spark, our love's pure flame,
In that moment, my heart belonged to you, with no one
to claim.

8. Resentment Has Loved Me

Resentment has never bound me
From reaching you –
Instead, resentment has repeatedly
Pushed me towards you
To see – if you are well.

Resentment has only stopped me –
From embracing you anew with firm hands
And saying, "I love you very much."
So that you cannot again, in that old manner,
Rest your head on my chest and show affection!
It has restrained me –
So that, with false touches anew,
We do not shatter into pieces again.

Finally, I have understood this, dear –
I love you immensely
But 'Resentment' has loved me as its own.

9. Love Yourself

As years and months pass by,
In spring, leaves wither and are born again;
When the funeral pyre's fire subsides,
The monsoon comes and washes away the ashes,
Then you will remain only in the pages of memory,
Like a dried red rose,
Which someone keeps within a beloved book,
While another floats away in the drain!

Love yourself, O beloved,
In the darkness, you are only yours!

10. Endless Night

You built our dreams with so much care,
Then shattered them in just a flare.
If you had looked into my eyes,
You'd see our dreams turn into lies.

They burned to ash, a ghostly sight,
Our future lost in endless night.

11. Illusion

Nobody loved me like you did,
Nobody wanted me like you did,
But fate kept us apart,
Banny, You'll remain the illusion of my life,
Seeing you happy brings me joy,
This is all I wish, Be happy for my sake.

12. Unnamed poems and Wandering souls

Winter leaves the city, covering it in misty dawn,
Abandoning the tender embrace of slumber's early morn.

I can't recall the last time rain kissed my skin,
Since losing you, memories have faded deep within.

In the Dusty sky, Copper stars softly gleam,
Forgotten nicknames and whispers drift through a
dream.
Did you, with closed eyes, ever yearn for something
more?
I, forsaking all, sought you as twilight poured.

Clouds amass upon the windowpane in evening's
sorrowed hue,
I'll immerse myself in downpours as dusk bids adieu.
Do you, too, weep silently, dreading the lonely night?
Inhaling deeply, do you conceal your sorrows out of
sight?

Yet, habit draws me to your vacant door once more,
Unnamed poems gather where paths cross and explore.
Wandering souls traverse streets as darkness descends,
In search of love, they vanish, leaving traces in the wind.

13. Burning Bright

In silent depths where shadows grow,
A weary heart bends soft and low.
Yet even there, a whisper stays,
Love's small ember, steady blaze.

The night may press with heavy hands,
Hope may fade like shifting sands.
But deep within, a fire ignites,
A soul unbroken, burning bright.

So take a breath, stand tall again,
Let love mend the weight of pain.
For through the dark, through rise and fall,
You are light—you have it all.

14. A Hope

In the dark, I search for you,
A flicker of light, a hope still true.
Your face lingers in shattered dreams,
While demons pull at broken seams.
Scarred but standing, I won't break,
Though monsters rise and shadows take.
Your warmth, your light, my guiding stay,
Through you, I'll find my destined way.

15. Healing wounds

Two souls met in quiet pain,
Healing wounds like summer rain.
Fingers traced a fragile spark,
Love was born, then torn apart.

A fire burned, then turned to ash,
Yet some flames refuse to pass.
A choice was made, a road was drawn,
Still, one waits as night meets dawn.

No chains remain, no anger stays,
Just love that lingers, lost in haze.
May joy embrace the path now set,
While silent hearts refuse to forget.

16. Silent Words

Do silent words still make a sound,
Or fade to dust without a trace?

The sky shudders with unheard cries,
Tears gather, shaping clouds in place.
Deep in the chest, where sorrow stays,
The fog-drenched night whispers its name.

Even beneath the golden light,
Shadows creep where memories frame.
Holding the path of love once known,
The heart longs for dawns now gone.

A poem penned in quiet words,
The heart still reads, though none may hear.
Perhaps it will remain unspoken,
Yet love still flows, silent and clear.

17. My Obsession

A fire lit my eyes when you,
In secret, with tender care,
Held the spoon and fed me love,
Or in the crowd, pulled me close,
Sealing my soul with a kiss!

A fire lit my eyes—
To love you fiercely,
To hold you tight,
So no dark shadow
Could touch your enchanting face!

Even now, that fire remains,
I sit alone in its glow,
Turning the pages of our past,
Where memories still breathe,
Deep within my soul!

18. Love's Hollow Remains

Where excuses grow and rise,
Accusations wear a shroud disguise,
Then know this truth, accept it whole,
Love has lost its heart and soul.

Where words are weighed in debts unpaid,
Echoes chase the past, afraid,
Where silence speaks in quiet despair,
And love dissolves into the air.

Where touch feels cold, no warmth remains,
Eyes hold no trace of love's old pain,
Where the fear of loss has turned to dust,
And memories fade beneath mistrust.

There, love is but a fleeting haze,
A lost night's touch in endless maze.

www.ingramcontent.com/pod-product-compliance
Lightning Source LLC
La Vergne TN
LVHW050250200726

843509LV00015B/2960